Climbing Out of Your Despair with God's Promises: Hope and Encouragement

By Laureen Giorgio

Co-Host of Living with Victory Radio Podcast
Co-Founder Living with Victory Ministries, Inc.

Making a Difference – Changing Lives

This book can be used as a ***teaching tool*** in Life Groups or anywhere people meet to study God's Word. Below are some suggestions. Who do you know that would benefit from this book?

This book was written to be given to anyone you know who is hurting and in need of healing—whether physical, mental, or emotional. God is the Complete Healer. Sharing this book will give comfort and hope. It will encourage people to trust God because He is Truth and Love. He is Faithful.

Give Hope of a New Life

Give a Book to a Co worker

Nursing Home/Hospital

Life Group

In today's world, God's Word is the answer to every problem. We need to absorb His Word into our souls.

Dedication

This book is dedicated to my grandmother for leaving me a legacy of faith in Jesus. Her determination and
perseverance led her to build her church for the Lord,
regardless of the obstacles she faced. Her example showed
me how to persevere in the darkest times of my life; and to
my mother, who gave me what her mom taught her.
They taught me that when Jesus is with me, there is no
reason for fear or despair. I just grab His hand and keep
going!
Thank you, Grandma and Mom!

Acknowledgments

This book would not have been possible without the support and encouragement of our wonderful audience. Let's include some warm regards from our podcast family members and pay them our deep gratitude.

"In God's Promises, Laureen Giorgio presents Scripture as the foundational source to meet our every need. She declares Biblical truth and gives examples for that truth through rich life experiences with which we can connect oh so well. When you find yourself or those in your life in need of trustworthy encouragement and wisdom, you can count on God's Promises."

Jim Kirkland, Executive Director, Audio Ministry – Billy Graham Evangelistic Association Blue Ridge Broadcasting

"Good Morning & God Bless,

Just wanted to take a moment to let you know how much I enjoy listening to you. Your personal stories mean so much. They inspire me in the way that it lets me know we are all the same with the same struggles. I love to see God at work in your lives. You are simple, kindhearted people that I find truly refreshing. I love the way you are so kind to one another as well. Thank you for your broadcast and the blessings you give others in your struggles. All Glory to God! May God continue to bless you both!

Your Sister in Christ, N.M., South Africa

"I love your ministry. The two of you are doing a mighty work for the Lord. You are great role models with much wisdom for us younger generation. Keep up the great work. God bless you immensely!"

Mike, Michigan

As Phyllis said, a very special couple! We were heavily involved with helping the families with hurt kids when I met you two, then I just added to my learning on helping people by getting to know you and watching all your action! We love you two, most of Central Florida loves you, and those who don't remember are just too young to know all the good you have done. May God bless you again and again as you fight your own day to day battles. I am praying for you every day, and hope you both hold up well as you go about your good deeds, and give love to all those you meet. Love you both!

Ken & Phyllis Hudson

President

Global Power Reduction, Inc.

Sanford, Florida USA

"Your show has impacted my life, and I'm grateful for your personal guidance and wisdom"

DM

"Donation in honor of the blessings your ministry has had in the life of my husband."

RH

About the Author

Laureen is Co-Founder, with her husband,
Tony, of Living with Victory Ministries, Inc., now in
North Carolina (formerly
Compassion Children's Foundation, Inc., in
Orlando, Florida, now celebrating thirty-seven years of service)
and Co-Host of Living with Victory Radio Podcast. She also writes a monthly
column in *Positively Haywood*, a local newspaper.

Laureen was born in New York, where she met her husband, Tony. They have
been married for fifty-four years.
Laureen's grandmother, Anna Marie Romanelli Lombardi (whom she never
met), left Laureen a legacy of faith in Jesus. Prior to being martyred for her faith
at the age of fifty-seven, Anna Marie founded the Calvary Temple First
Assembly of God Church in South Ozone Park, New York.
All her life, Laureen has lived by what she learned at Calvary Temple. Now she
and Tony want to share these same lessons with you through the pages of this
book—and through their podcast, the Living with Victory Radio Podcast. They
can be heard on all major podcast platforms.

Thank You, Family!

A BIG THANK YOU to my nephew, Albert Manachino III, who jump-started this book by doing the initial editing, and who encouraged me to make this book a reality. Another HUGE THANK YOU to my husband Tony for taking care of the details I wouldn't have had the time to finish. I could never replace the support he has given me over our 54 years of marriage. He truly is my soul mate. A special thank you to our Disney Family co-workers and all the volunteers, for always giving their time to volunteer when we were Compassion Children's Foundation, fundraising for a seriously ill child to receive their treatment. Their enthusiasm and love brought us together as one family working toward one goal: healing.
Love you all very much!

Laureen

Preface

**Climbing Out of Your Despair
With God's Promises
Hope & Encouragement**

*What a blessing to read through the episodes you seek to
place in the upcoming book. Laureen – your building upon
the Scripture with rich life examples made for
encouragement and thanksgiving and peace. Whew!*

**Jim Kirkland
Billy Graham Evangelistic Association
Blue Ridge Broadcasting**
Executive Director, Audio Ministry

All of our lives were turned upside down and inside out

when the pandemic hit in 2020. Every area of our lives was touched by these events, and people were in immense

despair, not knowing which way to turn. Lessons for living through COVID and any trial in life are found in these pages.

My husband and I were feeling the effects just as you

were—and still may be—of all the mayhem going on around

us.

In our Living with Victory Radio Podcast, I started doing programs with God's Promises to encourage you not to quit and give up.

This book is made up of ten of those episodes.

This book was written to give you hope and encouragement in your darkest hour. It is a book of Peace,

Joy and, most of all, Victory in Jesus!

His Words are the basis for the book. His Words are alive

and true. Reading these words prayerfully and often until His Promises become a part of you will change the way you will live your life.

Hopefully, this book will open your spiritual eyes to see

Jesus as you may never have seen Him before. Take His

amazing love into your heart and soul.

I want to thank Roy Harper and his team at Savvy Book Marketing for all of their hard work and expertise.

Also, a thank you to Amazon KDP.

Laureen Giorgio

Episode 1: Are Your Thoughts Killing You?

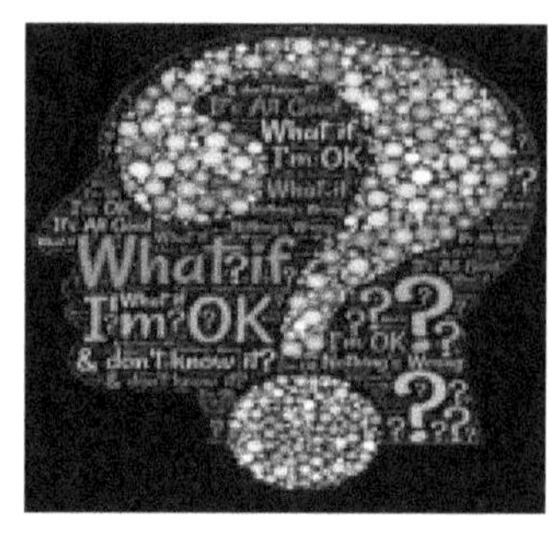

(Based on Psalm 94:18-19)
Life isn't always one smooth road, and we all realize that.
What are you thinking about? Are your thoughts killing
you? If you're feeling fear, anxiety, or worry, then you
really do need to try to change your way of thinking.
**"When I said, My foot is slipping, Your mercy and
loving-kindness, O Lord, held me up. In the multitude
of my [anxious] thoughts within me, Your comforts cheer and delight my
soul!"**

Psalm 94:18-19
That was David when he was fighting and running from
Saul. He was afraid of being killed, much like we're afraid
of being killed by this virus today. Our entire world has

been turned upside-down by this virus. Unable to see it and
fight back, our minds sometimes go off on ways of thinking
that are truly frightening in the face of all this suffering.
We can't see God, either, but we can feel His presence
and get to know Him, and he will fight for us. You can
know within your spirit that He is walking with you and
that He loves you, because, as David is saying, *"When my*

foot was slipping, your mercy and loving-kindness, O Lord,

held me up." When you stop thinking the thoughts you shouldn't be thinking, God's comforts cheer and delight the soul.

The quickest way to get your mind on God is to pick up His Word and start to read it. You'll find out who He is and what He has in store for you; that He is a merciful, grace-filled God who loves you and wants the best for you:

"For I know the thoughts and plans that I have for you, says the Lord, thoughts and plans for welfare and peace and not for evil, to give you hope in your final outcome. Then you will call upon Me, and you will come and pray to Me, and I will hear and heed you. Then you will seek Me, inquire for, and require Me [as a vital necessity] and find Me when you search for Me with all your heart."
Jeremiah 29:11-13

He wants you to come to Him. He wants you to tell Him all about how you feel so that He can comfort you.

"Then you will seek me inquire for and require me as a vital necessity."

Those two words—"vital necessity"—just stuck out to

me. A vital necessity, such as eating, sleeping, filling your

gas tank. You know He's vital to our existence, vital to our thought process. If we have our mind on Him, you'd be

surprised at the peace that comes. The anxiety and fear go

away because you realize that you're leaning on a

Sovereign, Holy God who has everything in control. He has you on His mind, and He's going to take care of you. But we have to first lean on Him and trust him.

That's the good news: We have a choice of what to think. We don't have to think about what we're seeing. Instead, we can put our eyes on Him. Remember the words of that old hymn "Turn Your Eyes Upon Jesus": *Turn your eyes upon Jesus, and the things of this world will go strangely dim.* Suddenly, joy will flood your soul when you know that He's in control and that He loves you, and He's got you by the hand. He's going to walk with you through this—*and you will require me as a vital necessity and find me.*

You'll find Him. He's not hiding if you search for Him with all of your heart. In these times, especially with businesses failing or going to the brink of bankruptcy, your thought process could be killing you. But remember: We all have the opportunity, especially in this age of technology, to seek God. All you have to do is go to the Bible. Make the Bible a part of your life on a daily basis, even if you only read it in small, digestible portions.

Remember the Lord's message in Deuteronomy 8:18:

**"But you shall [earnestly] remember the Lord your
God, for it is He Who gives you power to get wealth,
that He may establish His covenant which He swore to your fathers, as it is
this day."**

His words and thoughts should be your words and

thoughts. His Word is for our good; it is for our hope and encouragement. Personally, if I did not read the Bible every

day, I'd be in a total mess! Satan, the father of lies, will try

to fill our minds with all sorts of negative things—doom,

gloom, and hopelessness. But God is Truth. He cannot lie.

His promises are real.

If we are stuck on the daily news and all the

commentators on television, you'll be whirled around like

a top. But as the Bible says:

**"The Lord shall command the blessing upon you in
your storehouse and in all that you undertake. And He
will bless you in the land which the Lord your God gives
you. The Lord will establish you as a people holy to
Himself, as He has sworn to you, if you keep the commandments of the
Lord your God and walk in His
ways. And all people of the earth shall see that you are
called by the name [and in the presence of] the Lord,
and they shall be afraid of you. And the Lord shall**

**make you have a surplus of prosperity, through the
fruit of your body, of your livestock, and of your
ground, in the land which the Lord swore to your
fathers to give you."**
Deuteronomy 28:8-11

God has us covered—not necessarily the government, though everyone's trying their best to get us out of this

mess. But without our thoughts directed toward Jesus

Christ as our partner and our go-to in times of trouble, we

are brought to nothing. We do, however, have the ability to choose who we listen to and to choose to have God on our

side. We don't have to be stuck on the negative!

True, we can only see a limited amount with our human

eyes, but God can see the beginning and the end. I feel that His love and mercy are bringing us back to Him. He craves,

he wants, to have a relationship with us. God loves you! He died on that cross because He loves us. Don't just go to

Him when you have a problem, though. He wants to be

your friend, to walk with you in every circumstance of your life. Yes, we need him right now. He works through the

ones who are in charge. He will get us out of this mess. He

will take care of each of us individually.

To keep your mind and your thoughts elevated (and not

to give in to fear, anxiety, and stress), we need to keep our

eyes on Him. Sing a hymn. Learn to say the Lord's Prayer
often, and learn a few choice verses of Scripture, like Psalm
91, the "cheer-up chapter" of the entire Book of Psalms.
Just as He held David up in times of trouble, He is holding
you up. David knew he could receive the Lord's mercy and loving-kindness.
So can you. Look for the signs that God
does send us. We can't see those signs if our minds are
rooted in thoughts of chaos.

Though David was a great and powerful king, he had
his fair share of troubles: He was always on the run, his son

tried to kill him, he dwelled in caves, and he had enemies everywhere he
turned. Yet he wrote the Psalm that we read today. This is faith in action. So, with
the pandemic

crippling the world, we need to stop and realize all that the
Lord has brought us through, even when our backs were
against the wall! We must look at our past victories and see
what the Lord has blessed us with.
Shortly after Tony and I were first married, we
purchased a small restaurant. Little did we know when we
started that this would lead us to bankruptcy and loss upon

loss, in spite of our best efforts. We even lost our home. Nevertheless, the
Lord brought us through; the battle is

already won. Even in this pandemic, ***the battle is already won!*** Jesus
won it on the cross two thousand years ago.

When Tony was fourteen years old, growing up in 1950s Brooklyn, he was
involved with gangs. Leaving school one afternoon he was pushed by someone
unknown, and fell
head first down a cement staircase. He was unconscious
when he arrived at the hospital. He awoke to find a priest
giving him his last rites. He was surrounded by many people,

but he didn't know them because he had amnesia, besides lockjaw and a skull fracture.

He was made whole again while on the brink of death.

No one thought Tony would survive. It was the healing granted Tony by the Lord that brought Tony to life again.

Later on, around age thirty, when we lost our store, Tony again lay in a hospital bed—this time, with twelve blood clots in his legs. At this point, we were on welfare and struggling to maintain our physical health. Many looked down upon us and refused to help us out. Trusting in the Lord, we made it through that horrific episode. Today, in our seventies, we are probably healthier than

we've ever been, even though Tony may be in the "at-risk" category for contracting the virus—thanks to asthma. But

we're here. We've beaten several death sentences, including my breast cancer. God loves you. He gave you

life. No one on this earth—or even in hell—can bring you down if you believe and trust in God. It's certainly not easy to change our thought patterns. As we all know, it rarely happens overnight. But we have to fix our eyes on Jesus. When we do this, we see HOPE and LIFE. We know we are held up by an unchanging God, a strong God who is our rock. We must purposely take the hard road and deliberately change our thoughts, clinging only to the Lord for our help. He will never lie to us. He is all we need. Read his Word. His promises outweigh His commandments. Remember the two commandments He gave: Love the Lord your God with your whole heart, and with all your soul (your life) with all your mind and strength; and love your neighbor as yourself. When you internalize these two commandments, you will live a life of

peace, joy, and victory. You will know the Lord you're

serving. Whatever crises you face—no matter how horrific
things may seem—He has you by the hand. He's leading
you!
I know people are out of work and struggling to find

where their next dollars will come from. Tony and I have
lived this. We've lived with the struggle. We lived on
peanuts and lentils every day while we were in bankruptcy,
but here we are today! We are alive. We can honestly say
that in all the years we have served him, He has never failed
us. We don't have to be saints; he knows we're human. All
we need to do is get our mind on Him!

Tony and I joined an online Bible study group for

business people called Kingdom Connections, which is run through Free
Chapel, where Jentezen Franklin is the pastor. We've heard so many stories of
how our classmates'
businesses have been affected by the pandemic. They may
be somewhat worried, but the members of this group know who their Savior
is. We have a great time learning how
each of us can help each other. We learn that we're not alone in this. Joining
groups all over the world like this,
along with keeping handy a few favorite verses of
scripture, helps us get filled in a time of seeming emptiness. Do your best to
look out for someone else, too. Reach out

to friends and neighbors by phone or through the internet.
Pray for each other often.

**"For [then] He will deliver you from the snare of the
fowler and from the deadly pestilence. [Then] He will**

**cover you with His pinions, and under His wings shall
you trust and find refuge; His truth and His
faithfulness are a shield and a buckler."**
Psalm 91: 3-4

What a wonderful promise! (Look through the Bible

and find all of God's promises. You'll be amazed at what you find!)

Remember: Jesus is alive. If your thoughts are killing

you, read His Word. He is always your Father. Nothing will

end badly for those who believe in Him. Even if you don't

believe in Him, it's never too late to return to him. We have said it
time and time again: Jesus is your umbrella in the

storm! This is no mere catchphrase. We've had the Lord's protection
over us for a long time—and you can, too. Fix

your thoughts, your trust, and your hope in God.

Episode 2: Are Your Thoughts Killing You?

Psalm 91:14-16

When God makes a promise, there are two things we
must remember.
He never changes.
He is always faithful, and He cannot lie.
He is truth.

**"Because he has set his love upon me [God is talking
about us loving Him] therefore I will deliver him; I will
set him on high, because he knows and understands My
name [has a personal knowledge of My mercy, love, and kindness—trusts
and relies on Me, knowing I will never forsake him, no, never]."
"He shall call upon Me, and I will answer him; I will be
with him in trouble, I will deliver."
"With long life will I satisfy him and show him My
salvation."**
Psalm 91:14-16

I know, with my whole heart and without a doubt, that

these promises are true. God has been good to me many, many times
with healing in my body for various conditions.

Some may have heard this but, for those who haven't,

I feel it is worth repeating if only to give God the glory one more time!

Many years ago, when Tony and I were married for

three or four years, we decided to buy a fast-food

restaurant. I won't go into detail here. You can listen to

"The Battle is Already Won" for the whole story.

The results of a year's hard toil were losing the

business, the house, and everything that you would hold

dear materially.

It turned our lives completely upside down.

You might say we were having our own personal crisis,

as the world is having right now with the virus.

Crises take on various personalities. The stress and the

anxiety of the total unknown brought on pain in the left side

of my face that was unbearable. No medication could help,

and they wanted to cut the nerves in my face.

We were sitting in church one night, and the pastor was talking about a woman who had been sick for many years

and was never able to find help. When Jesus was passing

by, she knew if she could only touch the hem of His

garment, she would be healed.

As I sat there, I thought, Lord, if you could do it for her

then, I know you can do it for me right now.

That night turned into just me and Jesus having a long conversation. I told him I was pressing in.

I let Satan know that I didn't care how much it hurt but,

I was, without a shadow of a doubt, based on Jesus'

promises, receiving my healing.

I have to say the conversation was intense because the

pain was the worst it had ever been.

I just kept praising and thanking him for healing me.

Sometimes we need to do warfare.

I simply received my healing and said so!

On the way home, there was no change.

I couldn't tell you how long it took me to get to sleep

because of the pain, but I kept praising and thanking and

receiving my healing!

The next morning it was gone, and it has never

returned. That was over 50 years ago.

Since then, He has healed me so many times but, each

in a different way.

But when you are trusting Him, be ready to receive

however He chooses to send it.

This isn't a formula; it is just what verses 14-16 says

and what he promises.

This applies to any situation we are facing in our lives—

and especially right now.

Not to give up but to hang on to the promises that he

has given us. They're real today.

They're the same as they were when he gave them all

those years ago.

I want to impress upon you to read Psalm 91:14-16

because the promises here are so wonderful, from our Lord,

and so precious.

I just want to get it inside of you, to give you the hope

that this scripture intended for you to have.

Because he has set his love upon me—God is talking

about us loving Him—therefore,

"I will deliver him; I will set him on high, because he knows and understands My name [has a personal knowledge of My mercy, love, and kindness—trusts and relies on Me, knowing I will never forsake him, no, never]."

What a wonderful promise! He will never forsake us!
And this all goes to having a relationship with him
because when you really know Him, it's so easy to trust Him.

VERSE FIFTEEN SAYS:

"He shall call upon Me, and I will answer him."

He's not saying, "Maybe when I get around to it, or
possibly if I'm in a good mood, I'll answer him."

He's saying, **"I WILL ANSWER YOU.**
I WILL BE WITH YOU IN TROUBLE.
I WILL DELIVER YOU AND HONOR YOU WITH
LONG LIFE WILL I SATISFY YOU AND SHOW
YOU MY SALVATION."

OH, THAT'S WONDERFUL!
IT'S BETTER THAN GOLD, FOLKS!
Hang on to that.

Embrace it.

I just want you to know how much we here at Living with Victory Ministries care about you and love you. That's why we're doing this—because we want you to know that there is a living God who *does love you and who will take care of you, who wants to keep his arms around*

you.

So Just Remember: **JESUS IS YOUR UMBRELLA.**

Episode 3: His Grace Is More Than Sufficient

(Based on II Corinthians 12:9)

When God makes a promise, there are two things we
must always remember:
(1) He never changes because he is always faithful.
(2) He is true; he can never lie.

**"But He said to me, My grace (My favor and loving-
kindness and mercy) is enough for you [sufficient
against any danger and enables you to bear the trouble manfully]; for My
strength and power are made perfect (fulfilled and completed) and show
themselves most
effective in [your] weakness. Therefore, I will all the
more gladly glory in my weaknesses and infirmities,
that the strength and power of Christ (the Messiah)
may rest (yes, may pitch a tent over and dwell) upon
me!"**

I don't know what your particular need is right now. You
may have more than just one. You may need healing in your
body, or your need may be financial, or you are just anxious
and fearful because of the uncertainty of the future. One
thing I do know: I know the One who knows the answers. In
this scripture, He is saying that His grace, His favor and
loving-kindness, and mercy are enough for you, sufficient
against any danger, and enable you to bear the trouble

manfully.

With all honesty and personal experience, I can say that
this scripture gives a great promise to us who are walking in the dark right
now. I leaned on this scripture when I had my

cancer nine years ago. He was with me every minute, and I
can truthfully say His grace is sufficient. I leaned on Him
and relied on Him. Only He brought me through with such a
peace that I can't even begin to explain. I didn't know my
future or what was going to happen to me, but I did know the
One that I was trusting. As I said, that was nine years ago,
and again He has healed me. Don't be afraid to walk with
Him and trust Him. He will bring you through.
REMEMBER: JESUS IS YOUR UMBRELLA.

Episode 4: Delight Yourself in the Lord

(Based on Psalm 37:3-17, 23)
"Trust (lean on, rely on, and be confident) in the Lord
and do good; so shall you dwell in the land and feed
surely on His faithfulness, and truly you shall be fed."
"Delight yourself also in the Lord, and He will give you
the desires and secret petitions of your heart."
"Commit your way to the Lord [roll and repose each
care of your load on Him]; trust (lean on, rely on, and
be confident) also in Him and He will bring it to pass."
"And He will make your uprightness and right
standing with God go forth as the light, and your justice
and right as [the shining sun of] the noonday."
"Be still and rest in the Lord; wait for Him and
patiently lean yourself upon Him; fret not yourself
because of him who prospers in his way, because of the
man who brings wicked devices to pass."
"Cease from anger and forsake wrath; fret not
yourself—it tends only to evildoing."
"For evildoers shall be cut off, but those who wait and
hope and look for the Lord [in the end] shall inherit the earth."
"For yet a little while, and the evildoers will be no more; though you look
with care where they used to be, they
will not be found."

"But the meek [in the end] shall inherit the earth and
shall delight themselves in the abundance of peace."
"The wicked plot against the [uncompromisingly]
righteous (the upright in right standing with God); they gnash at them with
their teeth."
"The Lord laughs at [the wicked], for He sees that their
own day [of defeat] is coming."
"The wicked draw the sword and bend their bows to
cast down the poor and needy, to slay those who walk uprightly (blameless
in conduct and in conversation)."
"The swords [of the wicked] shall enter their own
hearts, and their bows shall be broken."
"Better is the little that the [uncompromisingly]
righteous have than the abundance [of possessions] of
many who are wrong and wicked."
"For the arms of the wicked shall be broken, but the
Lord upholds the [consistently] righteous."

...

"The steps of a [good] man are directed and established
by the Lord when He delights in his way [and He busies Himself with his
every step]."
Psalm 13:3-17, 23

***

Matthew Henry's *Commentary* explains that "These two
verses tell us to do good and to delight in the Lord which is
as much a privilege as a duty. This privilege-duty has a
promise annexed to it: He will give you the desires and secret petitions of
your heart."
Annex means "to attach, especially to something larger
or more important." When we follow these two verses, we
are attaching ourselves to something bigger and greater than
we are; we are attaching ourselves to our Creator.
Now I did look up the word annexed in Greek, and the

closest word to it (biblically) is *kenosis*, the act of emptying. It is the self-emptying of Jesus' own will and becoming entirely receptive to God's divine will. When Jesus walked this earth, He was a perfect example of how we are to live our lives; He did nothing without first going to the Father, and then He obeyed what the Father told him to do. We are to do the same thing: to delight in Him so that He will give us the desires of our heart. This does not mean that He's going to grant all the desires of the body, but He will grant all the desires of the *heart*—all the cravings of the soul. As Matthew Henry writes: "What is the desire of a good heart, of a good man? It is this: to know and love and live into God; to please Him and be pleased in Him. We must make God our guide and submit in everything to his guidance, and then all our affairs, even those that seem most intricate and perplexed, shall be made to issue well."

Verse five says, **"Commit your way to the Lord [roll and repose each care of your load on Him]."** You're taking it off of yourself when you're doing that, and oh, how free you will feel! Trust him, lean on him, rely on him, and be confident, also, in Him, and He will bring it to pass. This is a promise, and God cannot lie.

> **"And He will make your uprightness and right standing with God go forth as the light, and your justice and right as [the shining sun of] the noonday."**
> **"Be still and rest in the Lord; wait for Him and patiently lean yourself upon Him; fret not yourself because of him who prospers in his way, because of the man who brings wicked devices to pass...The steps of a [good] man are directed and established by the Lord when He delights in his way [and He busies Himself with his every step]."**

When we delight ourselves in His way, we busy ourselves with His every step; that means having a relationship with Him, walking and talking with Him, letting

Him know how we feel. After you let Him know how you feel, listen quietly to His voice as to what you should do. Finally, you must obey Him.

I do love these verses because I know we can trust Him to bring us through safely, and we can rest in Him. I know that I have His peace. You know that peace: the peace you can't buy, that peace that He gives; to know that you have all of this chaos going on around you when to be so at peace and at rest with yourself and in Him. To know that He is handling it and that you don't have to do all of this by yourself. He is in control.

You know, we go crazy trying to use our own human minds to work things out while He is sitting on his throne, and He knows all along exactly what has to be done. Now I will ask him, "Lord, just show me. I'm leaving all of this in your hands. Just show me what it is you want me to do right now."

He Remember, He is your umbrella. He has you covered. He's your protector, He's your provider, and does love and care about you and your family.

Episode 5: Love Your Neighbor as Yourself

(Based on Matthew 22:37-3)

***

"And He replied to him, you shall love the Lord your God with all your heart and with all your soul and with all your mind (intellect). This is the great (most important, principal) and first commandment. And a second is like it: You shall love your neighbor as [you do] yourself."

Matthew 22:37-39

"We must honor and esteem all men and must wrong and injure none and, as we have opportunity, must do good to all. We must love our neighbor as ourselves."

From Matthew Henry's *Commentary on the Whole Bible*

***

God created each of us in every nation. He gave us
different skin colors, languages, and cultures. In His eyes,
we are all neighbors. We are to love one another as He has

loved us; that is why He emphasized these two scripture verses because He wanted us to know that we are to love as He loves. But we can't love His way without loving Him first.

Hate destroys. Love brings honor and respect to relationships; these lead to peace and harmony. This is a great promise.

Episode 6: I Can Do All Things Through Christ Who Strengthens Me

(Based on Philippians 4:11-13)
Paul is speaking to the Philippians, and he is saying to them:
"Not that I am implying that I was in any personal want, for I have learned how to be content, satisfied to the point where I am NOT disturbed or disquieted in whatever state I am in. I know how to be abased and live humbly in straitened circumstances."
Philippians 4:11-13

Straitened means being hemmed in, or not having, in today's parlance, enough funds to "make ends meet." It also means that I now also know how to enjoy plenty and live in abundance. I have learned, in any and all circumstances, the secret of facing every situation—whether well fed or hungry, having a sufficiency and enough to spare, or going without and being in want. I have strengths for all things in Christ, who empowers me. I am ready for anything and equal to anything through Him who infuses strength into me. The word *infuses* means to saturate, to permeate, or fill me up to overflowing. I am self-sufficient in Christ's sufficiency.

Matthew Henry's *Commentary* says it like this: "We need God's strength to teach us to be content in every situation. In verse twelve, it sounds like Paul is boasting about himself, but he soon explains that his strength comes from Jesus through the Holy Spirit, who comforts us, for he is the Comforter, and he fills us with his strength and power."

As Paul said, he could do all things—not half, but *all*—because Christ empowered him. God wants you to know that He loves you very much. That is why He sent his Son to die for you, to shed His blood, and to take every sin—every sin that each of us has ever done or will do from the beginning of time onward—upon Himself. Remember that He is your protector and provider. He did not leave us here to fend for ourselves. He wants to walk and talk with us throughout every experience we have, in order to guide, empower, encourage, and give wisdom for every situation we face. When we go through our storms, we feel that we are alone, but this is far from true. When Jesus ascended into heaven after rising from the grave, He said He was sending the Holy Spirit, who is the Comforter. He said this because He didn't want us to face our storms alone.

This is a great promise,

and it is the Holy Spirit
who gives us the courage
and strength to face each
storm, no matter how
horrific the storm may be.
There have been many
times in my life when the
storm seemed to be
overtaking me, but because
I chose—remember: I said
"chose," because we do have choices, and it is up to us to
make the right choice—to trust what the Lord had promised
(that I would be able to do all things, even impossible things, through Christ
who empowers me), I knew beyond the shadow of a doubt that it was His
empowering me to do what
I had to do to get through the storm. To God be all the glory! God even
made a way.

When we find ourselves so hurt and tired that we cannot
pray because we can't find the right words to say, please
read these verses carefully. They are very important, and

they contain the best promise you could ever find. Do you think you are alone?

> **"So too the [Holy] Spirit comes to our aid and bears us up in our weakness; for we do not know what prayer to offer nor how to offer it worthily as we ought, but the Spirit Himself goes to meet our supplication and pleads in our behalf with unspeakable yearnings and groanings too deep for utterance. And He Who searches the hearts of men knows what is in the mind of the [Holy] Spirit [what His intent is], because the Spirit intercedes and pleads [before God] in behalf of the saints according to and in harmony with God's will. We are assured and know that [God being a partner in their labor] all things work together and are [fitting into a plan] for good to and for those who love God and are called according to [His] design and purpose"**
>
> Romans 8:26-28

I truly hope that you will take these verses and make them a part of you. They are gold.

Episode 7: For God So Loved the World

(Based on John 3:13-17)
"And yet no one has ever gone up to heaven, but there is
One Who has come down from heaven—the Son of Man [Himself], Who is
(dwells, has His home) in heaven."
"And just as Moses lifted up the serpent in the desert [on a pole], so must [so
it is necessary that] the Son of
Man be lifted up [on the cross]"
"In order that everyone who believes in Him [who
cleaves to Him, trusts Him, and relies on Him] may not perish, but have
eternal life and [actually] live forever!"
"For God so greatly loved and dearly prized the world
that He [even] gave up His only begotten (unique) Son,
so that whoever believes in (trusts in, clings to, relies on)
Him shall not perish (come to destruction, be lost) but
have eternal (everlasting) life."

**"For God did not send the Son into the world in order
to judge (to reject, to condemn, to pass sentence on) the world, but that the
world might find salvation and be
made safe and sound through Him."**
John 3:13-17

With all the danger we are facing right now, there is

something that is threatening you, and you have so many problems and so much stress and uncertainty about the

future, not knowing who's telling the truth. You just don't know. But there is one who tells the truth, and He never

changes. He is the same yesterday, today, and will be

forever. And His Word is gold, His Word is true, His Word

is genuine. He is trustworthy. You can trust the Lord; He will never ever fail you. I know He's never failed me. And in all

of my seventy-three years, with the battles I have faced—and there have been quite a few of them; actually, a lot—He has never ever failed me. His grace has kept me at peace,

even though it would seem like nothing made sense in the natural, and it seemed that everything was going crazy.

People thought I was crazy not to be worrying, such peace

did I have. But His peace will not allow you to worry if you just really put yourself in His hands. Totally put yourself in

His hands.

When I read these verses, I'm reminded of that beautiful

old hymn "Who Am I?" written by Rusty Goodman in 1965:

When I think of how He came so far from glory
Came to dwell among the lowly such as I
To suffer shame and such disgrace
On Mount Calvary take my place
Then I ask myself this question
Who am I?
When I'm reminded of His words
I'll leave Him never
If you'll be true I'll give to you life forever
Oh I wonder what I could have done

To deserve God's only Son
To fight my battles until they're won
For who am I?
Who am I that The King would bleed and die for
Who am I that He would pray not my will, Thine, Lord
The answer I may never know
Why He ever loved me so
But to that old rugged cross He'd go
For who am I?
But to an old rugged cross He'd go for, who am I?

It really humbles me that He would love me so much. I

know I wasn't born when He went to that cross. But I know

I was on His mind, as I know you were on his mind as well. The cross, the resurrection, and eternal life—who besides

Jesus can give you this promise and keep it? And what a promise! Be forgiven of sin, be made safe and sound through

Him. I love to say that. That means any danger or storms that you find yourself in now or ever will find yourself in;

through Him, you are totally and completely safe. Then on

top of that, He promises (another promise!) eternal life!

Wow! If that doesn't make you want to dance, I don't know what will. That makes me want to shout! When we give our

lives to Him in repentance, all of these promises become

ours, and our name is written in the Lamb's Book of Life.

Is your name written in His book? If you would like it to

be, say this prayer with me. And even if you've said it before, you might want to recommit, just to help your soul feel a bit

more at ease:

Lord, Thank You for shedding Your blood and dying on the
cross for me to save me from my sins. I am coming to You
just as I am and asking you to forgive me of my sins and
wash me white as snow. I receive you as my Savior and
welcome You into every area of my life. I want to walk with
You and talk with You all the days of my life. Thank You for recording my name in
the Lamb's Book of Life. I love You!

In Jesus' name, AMEN.

Now it would be great if you would
    just continue to read His Word, the
    Bible; pray, talk with Him; and follow
    His two commandments that He left:
    first, to love God with all of your heart,
    soul, mind, body; and second, to love
    your neighbor as yourself.

Episode 8: Are You Looking For a Good Hiding Place?

(Based on Psalm 32:7-10)

If you're hiding and you're not walking with Jesus, start walking and talking with Him immediately. That's the best
place to hide. The uncertainty of the times may have you paralyzed with fear and hopelessness, you don't have to straighten it out. The good news here is that Jesus will straighten it out for us!

***

You are a hiding place for me; You, Lord, preserve me
from trouble, You surround me with songs and shouts of deliverance. Selah!
I [the Lord] will instruct you and teach you in the way
you should go; I will counsel you with My eye upon you.
Be not like the horse or the mule, which lack
understanding, which must have their mouths held firm with bit and bridle,
or else they will not come with you.
Many are the sorrows of the wicked, but he who trusts
in, relies on, and confidently leans on the Lord shall be compassed about
with mercy and with loving-kindness.
Psalm 32:7-10

***

When we see the word *Selah* in verse seven, we should remember that God is asking us to pause for a moment, find calmness, and take it deeply to heart what we're told here.

When Tony and I first lost the store and he had phlebitis,

he chose to hide under the covers and not get out of bed because of how awful he felt. Can you imagine, though, what

it would be like to hide in the mightiest power in the

universe? Over time we learned that God is the best hiding-place.

Commentary on the Whole Bible, by Matthew Henry,

notes:

> *Thou art my hiding-place; when by faith I have recourse*
> *to thee I see all the reason in the world to be easy, and to*
> *think myself out of the reach of any real evil.*

When you're trusting God and resting in Him and in His hiding-place, you don't need to worry about the next five

minutes or if things are going to change.

All of us are in difficult straits right now and in uncharted territory. We do know the Source, who is Jesus. He was, He

is, He always will be. That's someone you want to be hiding in. Even now, in the midst of this pandemic, we can look for

God. No one can get us out of this mess. We don't even know where to start. But God is saying, "Come to me, rest in me,

hide in me; I will preserve you from trouble." That makes all the fear go away. The minute you start to think God is in

control, that He is Sovereign, you can relax, take a deep

breath, pause and calmly think about your problems and

Who has control over them.

You surround me with songs and shouts of deliverance.

You can have godly friends around you that are going to

praise and thank Him and shout for what's coming, because

He has it in hand. While you're going through it all, He will keep you safe. He is your source of help in a difficult

situation. He, and He alone.

You will preserve me from trouble. You may feel inconvenienced by what's going on right now, but you definitely won't feel the full sting of it. He will protect you. His arms are there to protect you. As Peter was going

through the storm, he had to keep his eyes on Jesus if he was going to survive. The minute he moved his eyes away from

Jesus, he started to sink. We must trust and keep our eyes on Him. Jesus will hold us up.

When going to bed at night, we are sometimes attacked by Satan and his lies. We remember how we're not raising enough money, or how our recording equipment is going bad, or how we're not reaching enough people, or that our podcast will fail. It's amazing to see what's happening, as our finances, slight though they may be, can cover our operations.

Tony often takes time in the morning to memorize some verses of the Scripture that he will repeat throughout the day. This can be a good practice for anyone to adopt. It can

remind us of how powerful God is, and how this Almighty Power can protect us. He loved us so much that He gave Jesus to die for us!

Nine years ago, when I was diagnosed with breast cancer, I knew what it was like to hide in Jesus. When I decided to do that, I felt as if I were in the palm of His hand, that I was so secure. He does not lie. It is hard for us to know who's telling the truth in the world today, but with Jesus near, we will know the Truth, the real Truth. His Truth.

He will surround you with shouts and songs of deliverance. He will send godly people our way to pray and give thanks with us. Don't isolate yourself! Look for godly people. Praise and thanksgiving are the most powerful warfare tools to have.

Satan just doesn't know what to do with a joyful Christian. It makes no sense to him that we can be joyful and praising God when all this mess is happening around us. But it's not your mess. God is working it out for you! You can easily go online, text, and look for these people. God can send you to a good church filled with good people who will make sure you don't go through your storm alone. You don't necessarily need hundreds of people. Just a few Bible-

believing, God-fearing friends will do!

All things are possible with God. He has delivered you

in the past, and surely He will deliver you again and again.

Nothing is impossible, and He is always the same. Thank

Him for what he's brought you through. When you decide to

fully trust Him and not waiver, you will get excited and be

filled with anticipation to see how He'll bring you through

this current storm. Only by exercising your faith and

perseverance muscles can you walk on the water.

I [the Lord] *will instruct you and teach you in the way*

you should go; I will counsel you with my eye upon you. God Himself is going to show you if you should go left or right,

but we must pay attention. We must have a personal

relationship with Him. We have to be praying and, if

necessary, fasting, and we must praise and thank Him and

have a constant fellowship with Him. This way, He will

navigate us through the situation. There is no guesswork

if you're listening for God's voice, but His voice is low. He

doesn't shout. You have to be listening for it, via prayer and

His Word. There are many accessible tools He has given us

to read His Word these days, thanks to the internet and social media. My husband, Tony, uses his phone every day and, at

the press of a button, he can access the Bible and Bible-based lesson plans, and feed himself spiritually.

Remember David's story and the trials he endured,

when, as with a pandemic, he lost so much. Nevertheless,

David fell on his face before God every time, and he came

out victorious. It wasn't easy. He felt depression and anxiety

as we do. But he knew where to go. The Bible is the ultimate

self-help book.

You are never alone. Just ask, and Jesus will give you

wisdom and guide you. His promises here should encourage you, so what is there to truly worry about?

Be not like the horse or the mule, which lack understanding, which must have their mouths held firm with bridle and bit, or else they will not come with you. God doesn't want to have to pull us in the right direction. He wants us to love Him and trust Him and to follow His direction in love and faith. We do this by cultivating our relationship with Him every day. God gave us free will to choose who our help is. He is there. It's up to us to ask Him. *Many are the sorrows of the wicked, but he who trusts in, relies on,* and *confidently leans on the Lord shall be compassed about with mercy* and *with loving kindness.* Here's another great promise! Be assured that God is listening, and that He cares for us. He will help you. You're not just speaking words into the air when you're talking to Him. He wants to fulfill His promises to you. The God who created us, who sent his Son to die on the cross and suffer so much torment, has given us an abundance of promises.

These four verses of Psalm 32:7-10 give us the substance of who our God, our Father, *really* is! Remember:

> He will hide you when trouble comes, and He'll soften the sting;
> He will surround you with people who will thank and praise Him with you;
> He will teach you and show you, step by step, what you need to do to get through your struggles;
> He will compass those who choose to trust and rely on Him with mercy and loving kindness.

God *is* mercy and loving kindness!

Also, remember that God left His Holy Spirit with us when He left this world. The Holy Spirit is your direct connection to God. He won't leave you. When you received Jesus, He came to live inside of you. "Greater is He that is in you than he that is in the world." We can tell you that these things will pass. If you follow God, things will work out according to His timetable, not necessarily yours. We've been through many problems and have learned to go through them with peace, joy, and victory. That victory is ours already because of His death on the cross.

In our thirty-seven years of advocacy in Orlando, we've seen the sufferings of so many who've dealt with devastating situations. We have, also, seen the hand of God at work in these families, whose children dealt with many different types of cancers. The faith of these families withstood the horrors of these diseases, knowing that Jesus walked with them every step of the way. The peace He gives is unexplainable. His Grace helps you through the most difficult of circumstances.

Jesus went through it all. He was beaten, tortured and crucified for you and me. He's our Champion. Choosing to follow Him will never disappoint you. Nothing on this earth will satisfy you. The media will not. But Jesus can and will satisfy you, as well as protect and provide for you.

He is your umbrella in the storm!

Episode 9: The Lord Shall Guide You Continually and Satisfy You in Drought and in Dry Places

(Based on Isaiah 53:10-11)

*Our choices can bring us either heartache or dead ends, or
they can bring us joy and God's blessings. When we choose
to follow God's commandments, He never fails to reward us.*

**"And if you pour out that with which you sustain your
own life for the hungry and satisfy the need of the
afflicted, then shall your light rise in darkness, and your obscurity and
gloom become like the noonday."**

**"And the Lord shall guide you continually and satisfy
you in drought and in dry places and make strong your
bones. And you shall be like a watered garden and like
a spring of water whose waters fail not."**

Isaiah 53:10-11

These verses reflect God's love and favor toward us
when we love and care for those in need. We look at what

we have, and we think we don't have enough to share. But when we are willing to share and do it with our whole heart,

that's when God's Favor showers our lives with blessings.

We've had His Favor for so many years. During this devastating time period, there have been many blessings—

they come in all forms; it may not be what you want, but it's what God knows you need. The best kinds of rewards are the

ones God gives you that you don't realize you needed.

Just before the pandemic hit, we took a trip to Orlando,

Florida, for PodFest, a major podcasting convention.

Initially, we didn't think we needed to go because we were

new to podcasting, and we didn't have the resources to make the trip. Suddenly, however, we won two tickets to the

convention. A major donor also paid for the trip—and did so unsolicited, no less!

And if you pour out that with which you sustain your
own life for the hungry and satisfy the need of the afflicted,
then shall your light rise in darkness, and your obscurity and gloom become like
the noonday.

God does reward! Now Matthew Henry's *Commentary*:
We must draw out our soul to the hungry *(v. 10), not only*
draw out the money and reach forth the hand, but do this
from the heart, heartily, and without grudging, from a
principle of compassion and with a tender affection to such
as we see to be in misery. Let the heart go along with the
gift; for God loves a cheerful giver, and so does a poor man
too.

We've all been so down at times that we have to look up
just to be even with the ground. If someone comes along at

these times and throws money at you or brings you a half-cooked meal, it is plain that they're probably not truly

interested in you. But if they go over to you and sit and show time and love, giving you something even mundane and practical, it shows that they care about your plight. It's in the intent; it's not something you had to do for the church or the organization or something you were forced into because you don't want to look bad. It's got to come from the heart.

This reminds me of the story of
two-year-old Mikaela, a young girl
we helped several years ago through
our Compassion Children's Foundation, based out of Orlando.
Mikaela had a few holes in her heart,
and she and her family were living in
Trinidad. In order for the surgery to
take place, they would have to make it to the United States.
Her uncle lived in Orlando and, knowing our organization,
he contacted us to see if we could find a way to get Mikaela
to the United States for the surgery.
We jumped on the case. Come Labor Day, we got
Mikaela to the U.S., and doctors and nurses at a hospital
agreed to do the surgery free of charge. They gave from the heart. When they saw Mikaela for the first time, they wept
because Mikaela didn't even have the energy to crawl.
The rewards that God gives you! Twenty years later, we received a call from Mikaela; she thanked us for helping her
so long ago. She didn't even know where we lived at the
time, but she found us. We kept in touch for some time afterward, and we truly got more back than we gave.

"They shall find God their bountiful rewarder and what

**they lay out in works of charity shall be abundantly
made up to them. God will surprise them with the
return of mercy after great affliction..."**

Everyone has something they're going through,

especially during this pandemic. God is still with us—and

we're living proof. Tony has respiratory problems, and we're both in the "at-risk" category. Nonetheless, we are blessed.

Do not give up. Know that God loves you and that he

rewards you when we do right by Him. He looks at the heart. He will always come through for you. You may feel like

you're a nobody, that you're invisible. You're not invisible

to God, however, because He created you.

***

**"...thy light shall rise in obscurity..."
v.10**

Tony's father, John Giorgio, a handyman at one of the

major condominiums on New York's West Side, always

gave from the heart. Everyone in the complex loved him. He would help the maids and housekeepers do their chores. He

even volunteered to help direct traffic in the city during a

fire. To thank his father for all he did, the silent film star

Lillian Gish invited him and Tony to lunch at Miss Gish's penthouse. During lunch, a stunned Tony asked his father:

"Do you realize who she is?!" His father replied, "She was a very nice person who may have been involved with movies."

This was certainly a God thing. There was no pity on

Miss Gish's part. She thought so highly of what he had done for her. When he died, Miss Gish sent flowers and cards.

He also conversed with all of the tenants in the building,

including Chester Morris, the star of the old *Boston Blackie*

serial, and the two seemed like lifelong pals. All along, however, he was unaware of Chester Morris's star status.

John Giorgio was, you might say, an "obscure person."

He was busy every day carrying out trashcans, cleaning up messes, and doing seemingly menial tasks. But he did the work anyway, and he was dedicated. Who, you think, would bother to notice him? Nevertheless, although Tony's father didn't fully realize how famous some of the tenants in the building were, he treated them with love. That's how God wants us to treat (and give to) others. Race, class, creed— we're all created by the same God, and we're all equal in His eyes. Love equalizes everyone.

"Though thou hast been long buried alive thou shalt recover thy eminency; though long overwhelmed with grief, thou shalt again look pleasant as the dawning day...Those that are cheerful in doing good God will make cheerful in enjoying good; and this also is a special gift from God."

- Matthew Henry

God will let people see you for who you are. You are not an obscure nothing. When you're doing good and doing what God asks you to do to help others (doing it with your whole heart), people will appreciate it, and they will lift you, as Matthew Henry wrote, up to a "higher elevation" from where you are. John Giorgio always looked for opportunities to help others, regardless of what the cost was or what he would gain. He was certainly not afraid to climb ladders. (Tony remembers this well. When he was a teenager he was not a big fan of "hanging around" with ladders, but this is another story entirely!) When a neighbor wanted to paint the exterior of his three-story house but was afraid to climb the ladder to get started, Tony's father offered to do the climbing and the painting.

John Giorgio could not read or write but he knew how to show God's love. What a legacy he left his family, and what a lesson of loving others to such a great degree. Mercy is something we give and get back. When we give freely to others, God richly rewards us. That's the key. Don't be afraid to give others a smile, a visit, a phone call, a bag of groceries, etc., especially in these stressful times.

—-

Tony and our neighbor are always so busy going our own
ways that they rarely get a chance to talk, but during a snowstorm in recent years, when we had to leave the house,
he called to make sure everything was okay. He offered help. He made time to give. A bond developed this way. It's not necessarily the spectacular things that mean something to
another. Even if you are of small means, you can still find
ways to give. No matter how hard we're striving to stay
afloat with our small ministry and its operations, God always gives us a way to keep going. When we need to get things
done, the means seem to be there. God will give you out of your need. Our friend Christine drove by one day to get us
supplies and food, and we didn't even ask for it. She
wouldn't even let us pay for it.
The bottom line, according to Matthew Henry, is this:
The surest way for a man to make himself illustrious; let him study to do good. He that would be the greatest of all, and
best-loved, let him by humility and industry make himself a servant of all.
We cannot out-give God. We cannot ask, "Well, what's
in it for me?" We are accountable only to God, and He will
be the one rewarding us, not civic organizations or churches. We're in a stop-over on this earth. What really matters is
how God rewards us in the end.

***

**"And the Lord shall guide you continually and satisfy
you in drought and in dry places and make strong your bones. And you shall
be like a watered garden and like
a spring of water whose waters fail not."**
Isaiah 58:10-11
*"As a spring of water, though it is continually sending forth
its streams, is yet always so full, so the charitable man*

*abounds in good as he abounds in doing what is good and
is never the poorer for his liberality. He that waters shall
himself be watered."*
- Matthew Henry

Try to nourish and water others. You will have nothing
to complain about, regardless of your circumstances. Earlier, we mentioned
our recent trip to Podfest in Orlando. There
were twenty-five hundred people there. Unbeknownst to all
of us, the pandemic was looming on the horizon, yet all of

us came out safely.

Episode 10: Promise of Living for God: Eternal Life with Him

(Based on John's vision of the New Jerusalem in Revelation 21:1-7; 10-27)

You know as well as I do that we are living in a very unusual time right now. Unexplored circumstances are definitely surrounding us. I don't have to name them one by one; it's a frightening time. There isn't anyone who is not feeling any or all of the effects of these situations we are facing, no matter where in the world we may be right now.

We ask: Is there any hope? Yes!

Who has the answers? Jesus!

And, if they claim to have the answers, who is telling the truth? Jesus!

We ask: Who can I believe and totally put my trust in? Jesus!

I feel like I'm in a maze, going in circles. Is there no one to help me out of this maze?

There is one and only one: JESUS!

Are you beginning to see a pattern here?

**Do not let your hearts be troubled (distressed,
agitated). You believe in and adhere to and trust in and
rely on God; believe in and adhere to and trust in and
rely also on Me.**

John 14:1

Jesus is the answer, the only answer. He knows the end
from the beginning. Put all of your questions, all of your concerns, all of your
fear and anxiety and stress in His hands,
and expect to receive the peace you are yearning for. Read
His Word every day. Pray, and He will guide you through
your situation. He is greater and more powerful than
anything that is happening in the world. Remember: Greater
is He who is in you than he who is in the world. He is in total control, no
matter how chaotic those circumstances you're
facing right now seem to be, or how overwhelming that mountain seems to
be. He is the God of the impossible.

He's willing to walk and talk with us through our current circumstances. He's
not leaving us alone, not for one
moment. Now here's another wonderful promise:

**In My Father's house there are many dwelling places (homes). If it were not
so, I would have told you; for I
am going away to prepare a place for you.**

John 14:2

Oh, the benefits and promises that become ours when we become His. That
is a great promise!

***

But it gets better! I am going to try to describe, to the
best of my ability, the holy city, the New Jerusalem, as envisioned by the
apostle John in the Book of Revelation:

*Then I saw a new sky (heaven) and a new earth, for the
former sky and the former earth had passed away
(vanished), and there no longer existed any sea.
And I saw the holy city, the new Jerusalem, descending
out of heaven from God, all arrayed like a bride beautified
and adorned for her husband;
Then I heard a mighty voice from the throne and I
perceived its distinct words, saying, See! The abode of God
is with men, and He will live (encamp, tent) among them;
and they shall be His people, and God shall personally be
with them and be their God.
God will wipe away every tear from their eyes; and death
shall be no more, neither shall there be anguish (sorrow
and mourning) nor grief nor pain any more, for the old conditions and the former
order of things have passed
away.
And He Who is seated on the throne said, See! I make all
things new. Also He said, Record this, for these sayings are faithful (accurate,
incorruptible, and trustworthy) and true (genuine).
And He [further] said to me, It is done! I am the Alpha
and the Omega, the Beginning and the End. To the thirsty I [Myself] will give
water without price from the fountain
(springs) of the water of Life.
He who is victorious shall inherit all these things, and I will
be God to him and he shall be My son.*

***

Then in the Spirit He conveyed me away to a vast and
lofty mountain and exhibited to me the holy (hallowed, consecrated) city of
Jerusalem descending out of heaven
from God,
Clothed in God's glory [in all its splendor and radiance].
The luster of it resembled a rare and most precious jewel,
like jasper, shining clear as crystal.
It had a massive and high wall with twelve [large] gates,
and at the gates [there were stationed] twelve angels, and
[on the gates] the names of the twelve tribes of the sons of Israel were written:
On the east side three gates, on the north side three gates,
on the south side three gates, and on the west side three
gates.
And the wall of the city had twelve foundation [stones],
and on them the twelve names of the twelve apostles of the Lamb.
And he who spoke to me had a golden measuring reed
(rod) to measure the city and its gates and its wall.
The city lies in a square, its length being the same as its
width. And he measured the city with his reed—12,000
stadia (about 1,500 miles); its length and width and height
are the same.
He measured its wall also—144 cubits (about 72 yards)
by a man's measure [of a cubit from his elbow to his third fingertip], which is [the
measure] of the angel.
The wall was built of jasper, while the city [itself was of]
pure gold, clear and transparent like glass.

Now jasper represents grounding and stability; providing comfort, security, strength, and healing (something you're
not finding down here, but it's promised to you when we get
up there).

The foundation [stones] of the wall of the city were
ornamented with all of the precious stones. The first
*foundation [stone] was jasper, the second sapphire [**blue**]*

the third chalcedony (or white agate), the fourth emerald [**green**]...
The fifth onyx [**black**] *the sixth sardius* [**red ruby**], *the
seventh chrysolite* [**gold**], *the eighth beryl* [**light blue, bordering on
yellow-green**], *the ninth topaz* [**a yellow
golden-brown**], *the tenth chrysoprase* [**apple green**], *the eleventh jacinth*
[**transparent orange-red**], *the twelfth
amethyst* [**purple**].
*And the twelve gates were twelve pearls, each separate
gate being built of one solid pearl. And the main street (the Broadway) of the city
was of gold as pure and translucent
as glass.*

***

As beautiful as heaven and the New Jerusalem will be,
the best promise is this:
*I saw no temple in the city, for the Lord God Omnipotent [Himself] and the Lamb
[Himself] are its temple.
And the city has no need of the sun nor of the moon to
give light to it, for the splendor and radiance (glory) of
God illuminate it, and the Lamb is its lamp.
The nations shall walk by its light and the rulers and
leaders of the earth shall bring into it their glory.
And its gates shall never be closed by day, and there shall
be no night there.
They shall bring the glory (the splendor and majesty) and
the honor of the nations into it.
But nothing that defiles or profanes or is unwashed shall
ever enter it, nor anyone who commits abominations
(unclean, detestable, morally repugnant things) or
practices falsehood, but only those whose names are
recorded in the* **Lamb's Book of Life.**
Revelation 21:1-7; 10-27
Realize what this scripture says: God will be living
among us:

*See! The abode of God is with men, and He will live
(encamp, tent) among them; and they shall be His people,
and God shall personally be with them and be their God.
God will wipe away every tear from their eyes; and death
shall be no more, neither shall there be anguish (sorrow
and mourning) nor grief nor pain any more, for the old conditions and the former
order of things have passed
away.*

In the chaos of what is going on right now, where you
don't know who to believe and what is true, we have the assurance of God's
Word and His promises.

*And He [further] said to me, It is done! I am the Alpha
and the Omega, the Beginning and the End. To the thirsty I [Myself] will give
water without price from the fountain
(springs) of the water of Life.*

Is your name recorded in the

Lamb's Book of Life? Are you
certain that you will be seeing God
when you go home? Will you be
living in the New Jerusalem?
If not, we could say a prayer that
will assure you that your name will
be in the Lamb's Book of Life right
now, and you could take Jesus into your heart. You can let

Him lead you right to the New Jerusalem when the time
comes (and those who would like to recommit to Christ are welcome to say this prayer, too):

Dear Jesus,
Thank you for shedding your blood and dying on the
cross to save me from my sins. I am coming to you just as I
am, and I'm asking you to forgive me of my sins and wash

me white as snow. I do receive you as my best Friend, my Savior, my God,
and my Counselor and as everything that

you would be to me, in every area of my life, walking with
me and talking with me each day.
I receive you, Lord. I thank you. I thank you for wanting
to record my name in the Lamb's Book of Life.
In Jesus' name,
Amen!

Now just simply read His Word. Walk and talk with Him
by praying. Follow His commandments: to love God with all of your heart, soul, mind and body; and to love your
neighbor as yourself. Always go to Him before you choose
a path. Let Him guide you and lead the way to a full gospel church, online or in your community.

Meet you at the Gate!